PLAY THE MAN

PARTICIPANT'S GUIDE

PLAY THE MAN

PARTICIPANT'S GUIDE

Mark Batterson

BakerBooks

a division of Baker Publishing Group
Grand Rapids, Michigan

© 2017 by Mark Batterson

Published by Baker Books
a division of Baker Publishing Group
P.O. Box 6287, Grand Rapids, MI 49516-6287
www.bakerbooks.com

Printed in the United States of America

Library of Congress Cataloging-in-Publication Data
Names: Batterson, Mark, author.
Title: Play the man participant's guide / Mark Batterson.
Description: Grand Rapids : Baker Books, 2017. | Includes bibliographical references.
Identifiers: LCCN 2016051201 | ISBN 9780801075636 (pbk.)
Subjects: LCSH: Men (Christian theology)—Textbooks. | Men—Conduct of life—Textbooks.
Classification: LCC BT703.5 .B383 2017 | DDC 248.8/42—dc23
LC record available at https://lccn.loc.gov/2016051201

Some portions of this book have been adapted from *Play the Man: Becoming the Man God Created You to Be* (Baker, 2017).

Published in association with the literary agency of The Fedd Agency, Inc., Austin, Texas.

17 18 19 20 21 22 23   7 6 5 4 3 2 1

CONTENTS

INTRODUCTION

February 23, 155 AD[1]
Smyrna, Greece

Like a scene straight out of *Gladiator*, Polycarp was dragged into the Roman Colosseum. Discipled by the apostle John himself, the aged bishop faithfully and selflessly led the church at Smyrna through the persecution prophesied by his spiritual father. "Do not be afraid of what you are about to suffer," writes John in Revelation 2:10. "Be faithful, even to the point of death."

John had died a half century before, but his voice still echoed in Polycarp's ears as the Colosseum crowd chanted, "Let loose the lion!" Then Polycarp heard a voice from heaven that was audible above the crowd:

"Be strong, Polycarp. Play the man."

Days before, Roman bounty hunters had tracked him down. Instead of fleeing, Polycarp fed them a meal. Perhaps that's why they granted his last request—an hour of prayer. Two hours later, many of those who heard the way Polycarp prayed actually repented of their sin on the spot. They did not, however, relent of their mission.

Like Jesus entering Jerusalem, Polycarp was led into the city of Smyrna on a donkey. The Roman proconsul implored Polycarp to recant. "Swear by the genius of Caesar!" Polycarp held his tongue, held his ground. The proconsul prodded, "Swear, and I will release thee; revile the Christ."

"Eighty and six years have I served Him," said Polycarp. "And He has done me no wrong! How then can I blaspheme my King who saved me?"

The die was cast.

Polycarp was led to the center of the Colosseum where three times the proconsul announced: "Polycarp has confessed himself to be a Christian." The bloodthirsty crowd chanted for death by beast, but the proconsul opted for fire.

As his executioners seized his wrists to nail him to the stake, Polycarp stopped them. "He who gives me strength to endure the fire will enable me to do so without the help of your nails."

As the pyre was lit on fire, Polycarp prayed one last prayer: "I bless you because you have thought me worthy of this day and this hour to be numbered among your martyrs in the cup of your Christ."[2] Soon the flames engulfed him, but strangely they did not consume him. Like Shadrach, Meshach, and Abednego before him, Polycarp was fireproof. Instead of the stench of burning flesh, the scent of frankincense wafted through the Colosseum.[3]

Using a spear, the executioner stabbed Polycarp through the flames. Polycarp bled out, but not before the twelfth martyr of Smyrna had lived out John's exhortation: *be faithful even to the point of death*. Polycarp died fearlessly and faithfully. And the way he died forever changed the way those eyewitnesses lived. He did what the voice from heaven had commanded.

Polycarp played the man.

In this four-week video series, we'll explore what it means to *play the man*. Sessions 1 and 2 will focus on rediscovering what it means to be a man—the seven virtues of manhood. Sessions 3 and 4 are practical resources for fathers, helping you create a Discipleship Covenant and Rite of Passage for your sons.

REWILDING

Before watching Session 1 of the *Play the Man* DVD, read the introduction and chapters 1–4 in *Play the Man*.

Read, pray, and meditate on Matthew 19:16–20:

> Just then a man came up to Jesus and asked, "Teacher, what good thing must I do to get eternal life?"
>
> "Why do you ask me about what is good?" Jesus replied. "There is only One who is good. If you want to enter life, keep the commandments."
>
> "Which ones?" he inquired.
>
> Jesus replied, "'You shall not murder, you shall not commit adultery, you shall not steal, you shall not give false testimony, honor your father and mother,' and 'love your neighbor as yourself.'"
>
> "All these I have kept," the young man said. "What do I still lack?"

Write down your reflections. Like the rich young ruler, is there anything you're holding back? Is there something missing from your relationship with Christ?

_____

_____

_____

_____

_____

_____

_____

_____

_____

_____

_____

_____

_____

_____

_____

_____

_____

_____

_____

_____

_____

_____

WATCH SESSION 1.

Video Notes

As you watch the video for Session 1, use the following space to take notes.

M+ 19:20

Rev 2:8-11

Discussion Questions

1. Are you a "tent guy" who likes roughing it or a "cabin guy" who likes a mattress and air-conditioning?

2. Polycarp was discipled by none other than the apostle John, his spiritual father in the faith. Do you have a spiritual father? What man or men have made the most difference in your life?

3. When have you felt most like a man? Where were you? What were you doing? What made you feel so manly?

4. Mark says our culture has left us "insecure and unsure of our manhood." Has that been true for you? In what way? How do the cultural and biblical definitions of manhood differ?

5. When you hear the phrase "man of God," who comes to mind?

6. Is there an area of your life that has become too tame, too predictable, too safe? How do you need to be rewilded?

7. Jesus was fully God, fully man. In your opinion, when was Jesus most manly?

Personal Reflection

In chapter 4 of the book, Mark shares the story of John Muir climbing a Douglas fir tree in the Sierra Nevada Mountains during a winter storm. Eugene Peterson called Muir an "icon of Christian spirituality." Muir was "a standing rebuke against becoming a mere spectator to life, preferring creature comfort to Creator confrontation."[4]

How about you? Are you a creature of comfort, a creature of habit? Or are you seeking out Creator confrontation?

Muir's vision was "saving the American soul from total surrender to materialism."[5] Like John the Baptist before him, Muir saw himself as a prophet crying out in the wilderness, crying out for the wilderness. His goal? To immerse everyone he could in what he called "mountain baptism."

Have you ever experienced a mountain baptism? If so, what did that experience teach you about yourself? How has it defined who you are, how you think about God, and how you approach life?

Take a few moments to reflect on your life journey.

When have you felt most alive? Most like a man?
How has your manhood been cultivated and celebrated?
Have you lost some of your manhood along the way?
In what areas of your life have you been tamed?
How do you need to be rewilded?

The rich young ruler asked the question "What do I still lack?" Can you identify with the rich young ruler? Is something lacking or missing in your life? Is there something that makes you feel like less of a man?

Take ten minutes to do a stream-of-consciousness writing exercise. Using the questions above, write your reflections.

_____

_____

_____

_____

_____

_____

_____

_____

_____

_____

_____

_____

_____

_____

_____

_____

_____

_____

_____

_____

_____

_____

_____

_____

_____

_____

_____

_____

_____

_____

_____

Personal Declaration

Make a commitment to play the man. It starts with rediscovering what it means to play the man. Then commit yourself to the process. Focus on making yourself a man—a man of God—and everything else will follow suit.

Take a few moments to craft your commitment.

_____

_____

_____

_____

_____

_____

_____

_____

_____

_____

Rewilding

_____

_____

_____

_____

_____

_____

_____

_____

_____

_____

_____

_____

THE SEVEN VIRTUES OF MANHOOD

Before watching Session 2, read chapters 5–7 in *Play the Man*.

Read, pray, and meditate on 1 Corinthians 13:4–8:

> Love is patient, love is kind. It does not envy, it does not boast, it is not proud. It does not dishonor others, it is not self-seeking, it is not easily angered, it keeps no record of wrongs. Love does not delight in evil but rejoices with the truth. It always protects, always trusts, always hopes, always perseveres. Love never fails.

Write down your reflections on the different dimensions of tough love in this passage. What are your strengths and weaknesses? Is there one dimension you need to work on the most?

_____

_____

_____

_____

_____

_____

_____

WATCH SESSION 2.

Video Notes

As you watch the video for Session 2, use the following space to take notes.

_____

_____

_____

_____

_____

_____

_____

_____

_____

_____

_____

_____

Discussion Questions

1. When you hear the phrase "tough guy," who comes to mind?

2. Share an experience when someone loved you when you least expected it or least deserved it. How has their tough love impacted your life?

3. Is there an experience when you lost your cool? How about a moment when you kept your cool?

4. Who has had more influence in your life—your father or your mother? Why?

5. Do you have a personal definition of success? If so, share it with the group. If not, define success before the next session.

6. Mark shares a few mantras his family repeats often in relation to the four values he wants to define his family—humility, gratitude, generosity, and courage. What values would you name as being most important to you?

7. Which of the seven virtues is your strong suit? Which is your
weak one?

Personal Reflection

Rank yourself from 1–7 in regard to the seven virtues of manhood, with 1 being the virtue you are strongest in and 7 being the virtue you are weakest in.

____ Tough Love

____ Childlike Wonder

____ Will Power

____ Raw Passion

____ True Grit

____ Clear Vision

____ Moral Courage

Regardless of how you ranked each virtue, is there one virtue you want to work on? If you try to work on all seven at the same time, it'll be difficult to see significant progress because you'll be diffused. Focus on one virtue at a time, and give yourself a time line. Then put together an action plan with measurable goals and next steps.

When Benjamin Franklin was twenty years old, he said, "It was about this time I conceived the bold and arduous project of arriving at moral perfection. I wished to live without committing any fault at any time; I would conquer all that either natural inclination, custom, or company might lead me into."[6]

After identifying the thirteen virtues he'd focus on, Franklin went to work on *one virtue at a time*. He made a chart and did a daily self-examination. I'd recommend getting a journal in which you can track your progress. While focusing on that virtue, come up with a reading plan. Read books that keep you focused on that virtue and challenge you to cultivate it. Use an online concordance such as BibleGateway.com, BibleHub.com, or YouVersion.com to search Scripture for verses on love or wonder or will power or courage, then memorize and meditate on these verses.

What is the first virtue you want to focus on? Write it down. Then write out a prayer. The seven virtues can't be manufactured by human effort. They require God's help. So ask for it in writing.

_____

_____

_____

_____

_____

_____

_____

_____

_____

_____

_____

_____

_____

Personal Declaration

Follow the steps that Mark outlines for a vision retreat. If you can, go on a retreat, even if it's just twenty-four hours. Meditate on the seven virtues. Then follow the steps Mark outlines. Write out your vision for your marriage and your family.

_____

_____

_____

_____

_____

_____

_____

_____

_____

_____

_____

_____

_____

_____

_____

_____

_____

_____

_____

_____

_____

_____

_____

_____

_____

_____

_____

_____

BE A MAN!

Before watching Session 3, read
chapters 8–9 in *Play the Man*.

Read, pray, and meditate on Malachi 4:6:

He will turn the hearts of fathers to their children and the hearts of children to their fathers. Otherwise, I will come and strike the land with a curse.[7]

Write down your reflections.

_____

_____

_____

_____

_____

_____

_____

_____

_____

_____

_____

_____

_____

_____

_____

_____

_____

_____

_____

_____

_____

_____

_____

_____

_____

_____

_____

WATCH SESSION 3.

Video Notes

As you watch the video for Session 3, use the following space to take notes.

_____

_____

_____

_____

_____

_____

_____

_____

_____

_____

_____

Discussion Questions

1. How would you describe your relationship with your father?

2. What is one character trait you saw in your father that you want to emulate?

3. Did your father *disciple* you or *discipline* you?

4. Do you have a spiritual father? If so, how has he influenced your life?

6. Do you see yourself as a priest, a prophet, to your family?

5. In chapter 8 of the book, Mark addresses the need to have good boundaries in life. Are there boundaries that you need to re-establish in your marriage? In your family? In your workplace?

7. Are you good at recognizing teachable moments? How can you become better at it?

Personal Reflection

Mark outlines the three challenges—physical, mental, and spiritual—in *Play the Man*. Using that template, craft a *rough draft* of a Discipleship Covenant for yourself and your son. (If you don't have a son, you can craft a Discipleship Covenant with a friend.) What physical challenge would stretch you? What would stretch your son? What books would make your "must-read" list? How can you model and practice the spiritual disciplines with and for your son? If you don't have a life goal list, start with setting ten life goals.

What men do you want to speak into your son's life? Make a short list of people you want your son to spend time with.

_____

_____

_____

_____

_____

_____

_____

_____

_____

Personal Declaration

Mark shares his definition of success: *when those who know you best respect you most.* Have you prioritized your family the way you could or should? Remember, saying yes to one thing is saying no to something else. Are you putting family first? Are you saying no to other things so you can say yes to your family?

What boundaries do you need to implement to put your family first?

_____

_____

_____

_____

_____

_____

_____

_____

_____

_____

_____

_____

RITE OF PASSAGE

Before watching Session 4, read chapter 10 and the epilogue in *Play the Man*.

Read, pray, and meditate on 1 Kings 2:1–4:

> When David's time to die drew near, he commanded Solomon his son, saying, "I am about to go the way of all the earth. Be strong, and show yourself a man, and keep the charge of the LORD your God, walking in his ways and keeping his statutes, his commandments, his rules, and his testimonies, as it is written in the Law of Moses, that you may prosper in all that you do and wherever you turn, that the LORD may establish his word that he spoke concerning me, saying, 'If your sons pay close attention to their way, to walk before me in faithfulness with all their heart and with all their soul, you shall not lack a man on the throne of Israel.'"[8]

Write down your reflections on what it means to "show yourself a man." How have you shown yourself a man? Where do you need to improve? What is the difference between being a man and being a man of God? If you were giving your son a "last charge," what would you say?

_____

_____

_____

_____

_____

_____

_____

_____

_____

_____

_____

_____

_____

_____

_____

_____

_____

_____

_____

_____

WATCH SESSION 4.

Video Notes

As you watch the video for Session 4, use the following space to take notes.

_____

_____

_____

_____

_____

_____

_____

_____

_____

_____

_____

Discussion Questions

1. What is the most memorable vacation you took as a child?

2. Is there a moment, like Mark's description of Sockdolager, when you felt like you became a man? Or you became more of a man? Share that experience and the challenges you faced.

3. What has been the greatest challenge you've encountered as a husband or a father? Share the mistakes you made or lessons you learned during that season.

4. After reading this chapter and watching the video, do you have an initial idea regarding where you might want to go and what you might want to do for a Rite of Passage with your son?

5. Identify a few "rite of passage" moments in Scripture. What can we learn from those moments and the men involved in them?

6. As you think about a ceremony to celebrate your son, where would you go? What gifts would you give him? Share your ideas with the group.

7. What are the most significant words—spoken or written—that someone has said to you? How did those words change the way you see yourself?

Personal Reflection

Work on a *rough draft* of the letter you'd like to write to your son to celebrate his Rite of Passage. What character traits do you see in him? What memories epitomize who he is, who he is destined to become? Are there Scripture verses you want to share with him? What values or virtues do you want to emphasize? Finally, what blessing do you want to speak over his life?

_____

_____

_____

_____

_____

_____

_____

_____

_____

_____

_____

_____

_____

_____

Personal Declaration

You'll never be a perfect father, but you can be a praying father. And prayer turns ordinary fathers into prophets who shape the destiny of their children. Prayer turns our hearts toward our children. Prayer begins to frame our hopes and dreams for them and, more important, the heavenly Father's hopes and dreams for them.

Take a few minutes to write out a prayer for yourself as a father. Then write out your prayer for your son. Try to avoid clichés. Ask God to reveal a picture of who your son can become.

_____

_____

_____

_____

_____

_____

_____

_____

_____

_____

_____

_____

_____

_____

_____

_____

_____

_____

_____

_____

_____

_____

_____

_____

NOTES

1. Leonard L. Thompson, "The Martyrdom of Polycarp," *The Journal of Religion* 82, no. 1 (January 2002): 27; Polycarp's date of death is the subject of much debate. It cannot be determined authoritatively, but I've chosen the date that best fits the facts, based on scholarly opinion and my own personal research.

2. Kenneth Howell, *Ignatius of Antioch & Polycarp of Smyrna* (Zanesville, OH: CHResources, 2009), 168–69.

3. Ibid., 169.

4. Luci Shaw, *Water My Soul* (Vancouver, BC: Regent College Publishing, 1998), 10.

5. "Why John Muir," The John Muir Way, accessed October 27, 2016, http://johnmuir way.org/why-john-muir.

6. Walter Isaacson, *Benjamin Franklin: An American Life* (New York: Simon and Schuster, 2003), 89.

7. HCSB.

8. ESV.

Mark Batterson is the *New York Times* bestselling author of *The Circle Maker*, *The Grave Robber*, *A Trip around the Sun*, and *If*. He is the lead pastor of National Community Church, one church with eight campuses in Washington, DC. Mark has a doctor of ministry degree from Regent University and lives on Capitol Hill with his wife, Lora, and their three children. Learn more at www .markbatterson.com.

Discover resources for individuals and small groups at

MARKBATTERSON.COM

You will find . . .

Sermon outlines

Church resources

Printable bookmark, flyer, and more

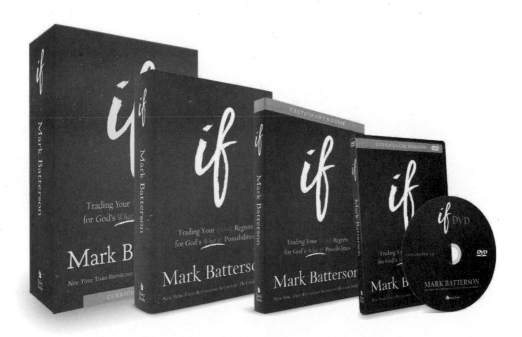

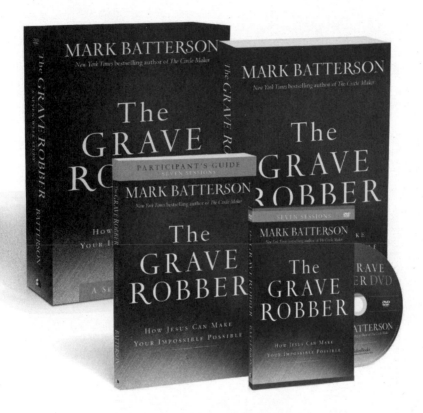